BRAIDED STREAM

BRAIDED STREAM

A POETRY DUET

JANICE REBECCA CAMPBELL

TONI HERINGER FALLS

BOOKS BY THE VERY IDEA®

Published by The Very Idea®, www.TheVeryIdea.biz
Book design by The Very Idea
Cover photographs by the authors

The Very Idea is a registered trademark.
PowerPoint is a registered trademark of Microsoft Corporation.

Copyright page continues on page 127.

Printed in the United States of America.
ISBN 978-0-9848673-3-2

DEDICATIONS

JANICE REBECCA CAMPBELL

To Toni
whose poetry expanded
my capacity for life

TONI HERINGER FALLS

To Janice
Whose heart is rich
Whose mind is clear
Whose spirit leaps whenever another
speaks the truth

CONTENTS

Part 5   ENDINGS AND BEGINNINGS   77

Part 6   WILD THINGS   93

BRAIDED STREAM

Part 1
HEADWATERS

We met through poetry

when we each read a poem at the 2008 "Awaken the Sleeping Poet" Poetry Festival in San Antonio, Texas. We liked each other's work, became friends, and discovered that despite our differences, our work often traveled over similar terrains.

Here are the poems we read at the Festival—the headwaters that later revealed a braided stream.

TONI

Tell Me

is your heart rich,
could another take

taste the full
of you
and all
you have become?

Is your mind so clear
another could know
it and come
away   changed?

Do you leap with
the arc of a fetus
in womb
whenever
another speaks

the truth?

If your answer is Yes
take my hand,

we will walk
in the present
together.

And when
our time here
is done

our spirits will remember

and go home—

I Could Have Stars in All My Poems

I could speak of
starry nights
star-crossed lovers
star struck
star gazers
star dust
stars that
shoot burn constellate shiver prick
fall
stars on velvet
galaxies of stars
star light star bright
stars upon which I might wish tonight

oh my lucky stars

I could take a mouthful of those stars
like burry marbles

and author the universe.

Part 2
CLOSE TO HOME

The road home

leads through small, mean-looking towns
despite friendly names   like:
Toad Suck, Possum Grape, Grubbs.

Ragged dogs in dirt yards
guard   rusty cars that ride on concrete blocks.
Leaning barns held upright   by climbing

vines   invite swallows to fly
in and out   through metal roofs peeled back
            like open tin cans—

pregnant bellies   the Ozarks shelter great—
deep lakes from which new-green hills rise;
dogwoods, redbuds, a grandmother's

quilt   thrown haphazardly over the mountain-
side—   hills flatten into
farmlands   brown bodies wet   and open—

waiting for rice, soybean, cotton seed.
In wet counties, trucks crowd around ramshackle
liquor stores   hungry piglets on a sow—

ghosts of sharecroppers' cabins lounge
beside the road, perch   on four stacks of bricks.
Flour sack curtains hang   in window frames; bare-

foot children play kick-the-can   in dust
—overalls drying on a line—
croplands give way to sloughs, Bayou De View,

river bottoms   where cypress trees hide the sun—
sit in stagnant water, knees drawn up,
where cottonmouths coil on limbs—and snapping turtles

wait—   Crowley's Ridge breaks the blank of flat
muddy fields   hardwood forests cover damage
left by quakes   tornados   Civil War—

hides   visions—of flint tools   burial mounds
hunting trails—   azaleas burn below white flowering

fruit trees, forsythias—glow in sunbursts—
purple bearded iris—   jonquils grow wild
long after homesteads become rubble   except
for chimney remnants   and robins who remember.

I travel the road home like a salmon lured to stream—

unerring   consuming   desire to be   where I
began   parents and their parents before   son and

his children after—   This road leads to home
built high   on ridge that was   deep forest.
          From window, I watch

mallards sail   early-evening lake   trailing lazy Vs
across   the still   surface—   lime-green tree frogs
cling to glass   the tiny pink, cupped

toes, white throats pulsing.   I watch
          the quiet beauty of this   homeland
          as it slips   into sleep—

The Din of the Culture
Drives Me Out of the Land

Underneath a snow-limned branch
the last red apple of the year dangles
while more snow drifts down
softly
silently

Ten thousand wildflowers
blanket the shores of a mountain lake
exhale perfumes
without a sound
in to the crystal air

A red slickrock trail
holds the heat of the sun on its back
beyond its final bend
Delicate Arch stands in perfect stillness
grander than ever imagined

Honeyed leaves
fall like blessings in the hush
of an aspen grove and I think
if I get to choose
I choose this for eternity.

The Year 2010

I.

See mother run; pushing twins in her double-wide stroller;
iPad open, on top of children's canopy. Diet Coke in holder.
Two black labs, tongues hanging—leashed to handle. She
seems to speak to me;

I smile, ready my tongue. No eyes meet. She continues her
Bluetooth conversation, running—running—hot breath of
day—snapping—at heels.

II.

See man in Brooks Brothers' wool suit, disguised as schizo-
phrenic at DFW. I see him listen. Speak to demons—perhaps
a lover.

Gesticulating. Stomping his foot—in polished Italian leather.
Hitting plate glass with palms, pacing floor as he speaks
silently—leans with open hands on terminal window—
head resting in-between.

Later, I see him staring silently across—the tarmac, shoulders
slumped, knotted hands in pockets, ear piece nestled in his
ear—a long-distance life, scheduled for immediate departure.
Gate 8.

III.

Husband and wife lie in bed. He reads the paper on his
Kindle. Watches vampire movie on new Hi Def-LED-
Flat Panel TV. She lies—curled up,

pretending to sleep, while mind checks off the day's list—
Washed. Shopped. Cooked. Cleaned.
Drove four children to: birthday parties, dance,
tennis, art, soccer, baseball, basketball. Changed clothes,
homework in the car.

9:30 p.m. Everyone fed. Clean, Asleep—in bed.
10:00. Usual sense of accomplishment. The need to
scream long   rumbling—in the back of the throat.

The New Car Has No Clock

The new car has no clock.
We bought the stripped-down model,
to save money.

Now when we look for the time while driving,
there is only a restful blank space
where time is usually measured.

Without reminders
of time passing or appointments pending
we relax
      cruise life's highway
          enjoy the scenery.

We bought the stripped-down model,
to save money.
But we ended up
saving time.

Ice Storm in San Antonio

I sit in a world that is mostly silent, except for the tired heater as it tries to warm this leaky house. My costume is comical—long johns peek from under wool pajamas that flare from a fleece vest. I wear my husband's hunting gloves, the ones with the fingers cut off, a knit cap that was jaunty until mice nibbled the edges. Space heater warms the area around feet, encased in Polar-tec socks and fleece-lined scuffs. I am warm except for a red, cold nose and the tips of numb fingers that turn white, then blue.

Deciduous trees hold up best. Eve's necklace, pecan, and walnut stand straight and tall, icy fingers pointing toward the sky. Even the hackberry—Medusa's head of limbs—is unbowed.

Hardy live oaks—laugh at the sun during our murderous summers. But the ice has them cowering. Heavy limbs sag under their own weight, each leaf encased in glass.

JANICE

Winter-storm-blown
Baccarat sheathes leaves, dainty
iceware dropped at dawn.

Small Sounds

My body whispers me awake.

Too soon it will rant—
render me deaf

to all other
sounds—
      bird song
      children laughing
      a neighbor's call

While I am able
I listen to the small sounds of dawn—
      a raindrop
      my husband's restful slumber
      the restive stirring of leaves
      —a squirrel under the loquat
                and finally
      the sleepy yawn of a dove.

Sunrise stirs darkness.
We begin again.

JANICE

Standing on this shore
with the sea pulling around my feet
I remember what it feels like
    to be drowning

The I Hate Toni Club *(1956)*

It didn't happen all at once. At first, teacher called on me—
and others in that sixth-grade class—to be runners, take
notes from the office to teachers. After awhile, I was the
only one he called on. Someone muttered *teacher's pet*. I
smiled, thinking that was a good thing. When the secretary
walked into our room with a note, I was out of my seat
before teacher finished calling—*Toni*. Too late. I noticed
mean looks from other girls, a glare followed by a note—
passed across the aisle. A secret whisper followed by—
laughter—all around.

When we studied Immigration, we were to stand, tell where
our ancestors came from. I told how Granddaddy traveled
from Germany. The next day, a classmate called me Nazi.
A knot of girls trailed me to recess, mad dogs nipping at my
heels. *Nazi! Nazi!* they chanted as I walked.

The ringleader told me of a club named—after me. *And
I'm the president!* she crowed. A gaggle of girls balled up
behind her, she stepped closer, slapped me. The group
circled, jackals intent on the kill. They pushed and poked,
Teacher's Pet! Nazi! I hate Toni! until a teacher broke up the
pack. Classmates melted away. I found my glasses in the dirt.

Next day, the secretary entered our room—with a memo. Without looking up, teacher called *Toni*. "No, sir," I mumbled, head bent over work. He glanced up, called my name again. This time, I stood by my desk and spoke, *No, Sir, I won't take it.* My voice broke. The answer louder than I intended. Some classmates gasped. He called another name, told me to stay—after school. When he asked, I said, *I don't want to be the teacher's pet anymore.*

Startled, a bit confused, he gathered himself, said, *When I say 'Jump!'—you ask me 'How high?'* then told me to write twenty times: *I will always do—what my teacher tells me—to do.*

Respect perched a moment by open window, then fled.

There's a Hole in My Wall

There's a hole in my wall
and sometimes when I'm groping
along in the dark
I find it
and peeking through I can see the world
I shout—I'm here—behind this wall!
and all the people flock around
      to marvel at the hole
But they know about holes
in walls
and plug it up.

Someone might leak out.

Wisdom

My body is a burden   my spirit must bear.

At times the weight of crumbling

bones
causes a tremble.

Last summer   when the roses faded
the body sank to knees
—old llama overburdened
not able to rise—   until
the load lifts.

How often can this spirit
be forced to ground
before it becomes

too tired   unable   perhaps un-
                             willing
to rise again?

And of what purpose to crush this spirit,
      one whose nature is to swell?

      Remember the early evening

we saw our first Magnificent
Frigatebirds? We sat on the pier,
day dying behind coast oaks. They appeared
like prehistoric pterodactyls.
Sailing high heaven—
calligraphy strokes on shadow cast
by a falling sun   birds etching an image
of that spirit to remind.

Snowy Egret dips
its wings in a pool of sky …
I feel the ripples.

Part 3
THE WIDER WORLD

The Other

Before the First World War, and still young,
my grandfather emigrated from Hamburg, Germany,
found work in a South Arkansas sugar mill. Later,
the foreigner was accused of putting ground glass in
the sweetener.

My German cousin fled her country during Hitler's
time, sought sanctuary in Switzerland for her two sons,
both blond, blue-eyed   perfect Aryans
except   the older was a Mongoloid.

This cousin's husband—a career army officer,
marched with the Third Reich to the Russian Front.
There, captured and held prisoner eleven years
—wife and children unaware he was alive, until
he walked home.

In the sixth grade, we told where our families
came from. I explained that my grandfather was born
in Germany. Next day, classmates mocked
me on the playground with jeers   *Nazi, Nazi.*

A teenager, I walked the grounds of Dachau—

sanitized.   Green grass, gold wildflowers covered.
But nothing concealed

                    The Ovens   or   the Smokestacks.

I stood   long after friends   moved on.

Seventy years after the genocide, behind a thick
pane of glass, a large pile of shoes
in the Holocaust Museum

still has a faint scent.

The Difference

Thirty-three people died by gunfire
at a college in Virginia and
we cannot get enough of it
we want to know everything about the killer
and each of his victims, about every
horrific and heroic act
while in this same world
183 people died in U.S.-occupied Iraq today
and we have no curiosity,
flags do not fly at half mast for them,
we do not mourn, nor pray, nor
wring our hands over the senseless waste.

The end results are the same:
Lives brutally cut short
families devastated
a society traumatized—

Explain to me
the difference.

Autumn Evening

Simple supper by the fire.
Flames under dried oak.
Bowls of Irish oatmeal steaming.
Fold in bananas, dry cranberries,
golden spools of honey. Butter pooling.
Toasted bread on a blue plate.
Sweet cinnamon.

>In another country, a world away,
>a different meal
>—one for the buzzards, jackals of Darfur.
>*Janjaweed* militias sweep into
>small towns, slaughter villagers because
>they own black skins,
>broad noses. Militias set huts
>on fire, flames lick thatched roofs, then gather
>around each surviving woman
>and girl—15 to 20 take turns between
>their legs—
>carrion eaters circle, wait
>   patiently—
>for simple supper by the fire.

>In a Darfur refugee camp

flies
prowl around lips
feasting on bits
of cereal, crusted there—

Listless children
bellies swollen tight
as melons
gaze with mute eyes—
too young to know.

Sterling spoon pauses on its way to my mouth.
Toast turns stale on chipped blue plate.

after NBC's 60 Minutes
October 2006

Fort Sam Cannon

BOOM!
Cannon shot from old Fort Sam Houston
echoes across San Antonio
like clockwork each morning.

We think
It's 5:30
and go back to sleep
not fearing loss of
electricity or shelter
or someone beloved.

This ritual

is a world away
from bombardment
that shocks Baghdad sleepers
awake at any hour
with the awful thought
Will we die tonight?

March Madness 2011

South Texas live oaks hold
leaves until winter's last breath.
Redbuds, Mountain Laurels rush to fill
ragged spaces with magenta and purple,

Lady Banks roses soar, launch
cascades of butter-yellow blooms.
Esperanzas, Mexican Birds-of-Paradise
grow back from the roots

remind that nature wants to flourish
despite devastation in Japan, continued
threat of nuclear meltdown, a seed
will sprout, push up through the wreck

—blossom.   Babies will hold
the ends of broken threads, will sing
the songs of the perished.

Young people in Tunisia, Egypt, Libya
realize Hope is not a plan—

fight to overthrow tyranny, shout

to gain a voice. Achieve in weeks
what parents failed to do in thirty years.

And in all this March madness
a Supermoon rises for each of us
Closer. Brighter. Reflecting a blessing,
                    repeating a promise—
the world is not without end
                    but until that time,
spring comes after winterkill.

Sunflowers

The directions were simple:
Open container lid.
Remove seeds from bag.
Plant 1" deep.
Water.
Place in a sunny location.

Within two days
roots, stems, leaves uncurled
from tidy packages.
Life became.

Who can plant a seed
and not believe in everything.

For Fred in Late Summer
Tuesday, August 23, 2011

Today we watch dead leaves
drift from the ancient elm, blanket
dying English ivy, brown Holly ferns.

In this unspeakable heat
the bird bath glows hot, white, dry   again
and our governor believes global warming—
          a conspiracy of scientists.

Today the earth quaked in the east,
people spilled into the streets, eyes wide,
fearing another terrorist strike.

In Tripoli, rebels entered Gadhafi's
compound, became revolutionaries
for a new order in a land tired of the old.

Beloved basketball coach, Pat Summit, stands
unbowed, faces another opponent
who will beat her, but not today.

A good man kissed his family, closed his eyes,
expecting to wake with a new knee—

during surgery, a vessel in the brain
opened, bloomed red.

We know, don't we, that nothing
can be certain—   especially tomorrow.

To quiet the fear

we pray for endurance, seek the shade,
remember humpback whales and calves
        blowing white spray
        lifting their flukes
        diving deeply in cold, silky waters

love every day.

Cracked

A fissure
flaw
in life
love
heart
hope
in the here and now
in the long ago
remembered
reconsidered
embraced.

The vessel holds.
We carry on.

Coast Live Oaks

Rockport, Texas

Today, I wander beneath
Coast live oaks,
grow dizzy following
trunks rising into green
canopies—
wonder at the impossible
twist—the turns they make,
growing   inandoutandback
                onto.

Married to land   water   sky—
Coast live oaks live—
only—on this short, narrow,
rocky bit of shore.

Thousands of years ago, seedlings
yielded to constant wind,
        grew into large trees that lean
inland—   motts of towering hedges
        sheared smooth.

Tropical storms. Hurricanes. Wild fires.

Carving names into ragged trunks—

        they remain
gifting   shelter   fuel   food
to   cannibal Indians   *conquistadores*
      Tejanos   pioneers.

These bent oaks remind of ordinary people
          bowed by life—
Katrinas   oil spills   genocide

Women lose entire families   rise from the mud;
men survive a father's fist   become tender parents;
families who can no longer fish   hook oil booms
      to shrimp boats;
orphans live in refugee camps, without an arm or leg—
then graduate with honor   run the race
make us humble.

JANICE

The live oaks of south
Texas dance to a slow song
millennia long.

TONI

We were all children

> before 8:45 a.m.
> September 11.
> 2001.

We had nothing better to do
    than bicker back—and forth—
                            at each other

Like my brother and me
    when trapped together in the back seat
    on a long family trip.

We'd draw an imaginary line down the middle.

Cross over the line—and one or the other would
    Whine Fuss Hit Pinch
    Upset the puzzle
    Break   a crayon
    until we brought down
    the equalizing vengeance
    of Mother's left arm.

                    ~   ~   ~

We had nothing better to do than

rage at each other from
our cars

cut each other
off—

scream
Crap!   *Idiot!*   *Get off the phone!*

set the bird free

We sought out Mother Media
    to air our dirt—
    gain support
    for our—side

We engaged litigation
    to settle our petty
    grievances
    against each other—
    to award us easy
    money—
    to prove our point
Voyeurism into—the lives of others
    seems to be our pastime
until the hidden waiting evil
    arm—
    of the fanatics

    makes a mockery of

their gentle religion

knocks us
to our knees

~   ~   ~

We watched as a people
    while friends held hands
    and jumped from top floors
    while the skyscape of the City—disappeared
    towers falling
    one—after
    the other

In our fear
    we fled   fought   froze

Watched heroes emerge—from dust
                                    clouds
    firefighters
    police
    passengers who

    aborted
    terrorist missions

And then we stood   up   grew up
    Discovered
                        our resolve.

Enlightenment

I've lived to see
Santa Claus debunked
and to know that childhood
was not the idyll my parents proposed
and I understand the purpose of education
is indoctrination and
deceit is politicians' stock-in-trade
while business exists to maximize profits
no matter the cost
which brings me to religion
which fell along with the Twin Towers
vaporized
by men of perfect faith.

Arrowhead

Held lightly in palm,
the stone cool. Weight
barely measures. Although it appears
to be a child's toy, my thumb
proves otherwise
as it slides
gingerly down the saw tooth sides. The point
draws a bead of blood.

Born in antiquity, the arrowhead retains
all the killing power it had
when shot from the first bow.

In light of blazing wood, Anasazi hands
chipped away
at this flint,
a bird's death
on his mind, or maybe
roasted squirrel—perhaps a rabbit robe
for boy child feeding at mother's breast.

What if he had a vision gazing
into flame—

looked forward into
our present?
Observing mall milieus, rivers
of cars, factories flushing smoke,
our obsession with having
everything now—might he feel
confused? Would he wonder, *How*
is it they came to lose
time, skills, patience?

I glance toward the arrowhead, warm now,
resting in my palm. It speaks,
What have you gained?
Does it have the same value
as what you have lost?

Turning a Corner

At the corner of Sonterra and Hardy Oak
      a tiny clutch inside my chest.

This is the corner where I spotted
a fledgling desert willow
one summer day two years ago
its pink bells
bouncing in the sun
      above a spot of wild ground.

On that day,
I parked my car
crossed a busy intersection
bent low to meet the little growing thing
eye-to-blossom,
      small, but on its way to tree.

On this day,
I see the ground scraped bare
to make way for a different kind of development.
A lone butterfly flits to find its bearings.
And I wonder: *What will sustain us?*
      How shall I live?

Small Town, Southern White Child

While I was growing up, my entire family
hired colored help.

They cooked our food.   Cleaned our homes.
Tended gardens   grandmothers' prize roses.
          Baby-sat when we were small.

All the help gathered in the background
on Christmas Day to receive
gifts—new shirts, pants, dresses, coats.

Sitting beside my father's mother, I heard her rant
about the help.   *They were*   *all*
stupid
lazy
unclean
untrust-
          worthy

In the community   I saw them
          use colored drinking fountains
          sit upstairs in The Palace Movie Theater
          attend Booker T. Washington school
          live in Colored Town, across the tracks

use separate restrooms
enter through back doors, side doors

Separate.　　Less than.

I　　also saw　　Billy　　work three jobs　　raise
nine children　　　　all graduated from college
—a feat my family did not accomplish.

Lee　　told fifty different stories
about how he lost his arm—
　　　　One day,　　*a huge, mean dog chewed it off.*
　　　　Another　　*an alligator chomped it right in two.*
　　　　My favorite—　*cut it off　　gave to a man,*
　　　　　　　　　who had no arms.

The truth—　　a sawmill accident when he was a kid.

Lee worked as efficiently as any man with two arms—
whether outside with a hoe　　or
inside with a silver tray.
When he got drunk and cops threw him in jail—
Grandmother bailed him out.

Ella—　Tall.　Straight.　Proud.　African queen
in starched white.　Let me jump
on　　her　　feather bed　　　　was never too busy

to grab me in a bear-hug,   smelled like lavender—
even when fixin' dinner.
Annie Mae   rescued my little brother and me
from neighborhood bullies, who had taken us to
the garage   to pull down our underwear.

Whenever I cruised her kitchen, pilfering food
before Sunday dinner   Gussie—playfully—
bopped this offending hand with any utensil she held.

*Now, Miss Toni, you git on outta ma' kitchen. Dinner
ain't ready yet.*

~   ~   ~

Mom and I sunbathed an hour   or two
each summer morning—   sprinkler hose
threaded under chaise lounges, Johnny Mathis
on the radio, *Seventeen* magazine in these hands.

One day, Louise asked *Miss Janice,* my mother, to
'splain somethin'.   *How come colored folk work
they whole lives   trying to be white   an' white folk
spend all they time   trying to get black?*

Stain

Against a background blue as Texas sky
one photograph of graft v. host disease
transports me, past all will, to time gone by—
or not so long, that such a thought should seize?

Calves, dark-skinned, above feet stalwart planted,
against a background blue as Texas sky—
and I see shackles clamped 'round each ankle
"a man enslaved," the mind stain does imply.

Not "Bahamian" barefoot on his beach,
nor "Masai warrior" out to prove his mettle …
with mind stained by a nation's early greed,
white v. black disease proves hard to battle.

In spite of roads with good intentions paved
both sides of this conundrum remain enslaved.

JANICE

To Paul Robeson on the Occasion
of the Inauguration of the
44th President of the United States

All I know is that within every man and woman
a secret is hidden, and as a photographer it is
my task to reveal it if I can.
—YOUSUF KARSH, PORTRAIT PHOTOGRAPHER

What would Karsh reveal
in a portrait taken of you
on this day
233 years after the founding
of a nation built partially
upon the whip-lashed backs
of your ancestors?

You, descendent of Africa's Igbo people
whose father escaped from
a North Carolina plantation where
he'd been born a slave

You, two-time All-American football player
who was declared the greatest defensive end
to ever trod the gridiron
Phi Beta Kappa valedictorian at Rutgers,

graduate of Columbia Law School,
attorney
whose dictation was refused by
a white stenographer because
of the color of your skin

You, who carried Shakespeare's *Othello*
to a record 296 performances on Broadway
years after starring in the play in England
when no one in your own country
would hire a black man for the role

You, conversant in 20 languages
fluent in 12
who found it possible to walk
in full human dignity
only in a foreign country,
whose U.S. passport was revoked
because you spoke out overseas
about the treatment of blacks in America
admonished that this was
a "family affair."

In a 1941 portrait by Karsh
your eyes burn with the full certainty

that you are five-fifths of a man.
Your shoulders are braced
in remembrance,
but not acceptance,
of your times.

What would Karsh reveal
in a portrait taken of you on this day
when the words of Martin Luther King Jr.
echo from the marble feet of Lincoln
up the Washington Mall
overtop jubilant crowds
to the steps of the U.S. Capitol—
where a younger brother
who has been judged based upon
the content of his character
stands in the full dignity of a man
free at last, free at last,
thank God Almighty,
free at last.

Part 4
THEE AND ME

Lessons in Love Learned
Watching Pee Wee Football Practice

Don't be afraid of love.
Don't look away from it.
Don't wave at it as it goes by.
Don't swing at it.
Don't fall on it.
Don't jump over it.
Don't bobble it.
Don't bounce it.
Don't bat it.
Don't drop it.
Don't let love slip through your fingers.

Keep your eye on love.
Reach for it with both hands.
Pull it in.
Cradle it close.
Run like the wind
all the way to the end.

Love Song

Sometimes
   when we lie
      together
         I move a foot or finger
            to remind me where your body ends
               and mine begins

Sometimes
   when a crowd stands between
      I seek your blue-gray eyes,
         find them looking—into mine

Sometimes
   you say the words breathing
      across my tongue, not yet spoken
         then smile knowingly as my mouth
            opens. Closes. Opens

Sometimes
   the music we make
      strings crystal beads on my lashes,
         I struggle with the great note
            that lodged, swelling in this throat

We spent spring and the summer of our lives sliding
     down separate paths, unaware those years prepared us
          for that day on your sailboat   when we
               split open the sky

I did nothing to deserve a walk
     with you through fall orchards,
          the crisp taste of shared apple
               juice running down our chins

and now we begin
     a bundled stroll into winter, snowflakes
          on our tongues and a lonely elk's
               love song on a frozen morning—

This Song

Two melodies
moving within a space and time
you and I weave in
      and out
sometimes discordant
sometimes in
harmony so sweet
the world stops
      shines.

We two
twined together
play the notes we know
      make music
sing this song.

TONI

Goodbye Died in My Mouth

The front's slate gray edge—darkens to charcoal. Pillar of stone.
I watch three funnels drop. My son—my home in their path.

Despite my uncle's cries to run for the storm shelter, I shake my
head, raise hand in goodbye. Eyes on the funnels, I gun the engine,
skitter gravel, barrel toward them. Rain erases the highway.
Flashes of lightning turn night-like sky—back into day; my car
and body rattle with each thunder clap. Hail cracks the glass.
Wind lifts the front wheels—terror drives this car.

The storm passes over—as I near home. Sunlight through thread-
bare clouds. On my street, limbs are down, but no trees. Home
sits safely in its cove of pines, glistening under ice. Scent of pine
needles, crushed. I race into the house, wild-eyed. My son sits
at the table doing his math. *Hey, Mom. Cool storm! Did you see
the hail?*

JANICE

A threatening sky—
wind chimes play "Stormy Weather"
the children scatter.

From a distance

you can't see he's old,
can't see—he's dying.
Salt air invigorates
a tired body.

He lopes across the little spit of land—
paws kick up puffs of sand,
not like the rampaging bruiser,
but an elder statesman,
the feel of Gulf wind
in his long brown ears.

Forefeet braced on bulkhead,
eagerly scans the water,
hoping a mullet will leap for light,

even as spray from breaking waves
shower him like
a benediction.

When he was young,
he flung himself from
the bulkhead,

began paddling to
Havana.

Remember going after him?
Pacing the shore as you waded
farther and farther out—
heads hidden by waves.
I thought I'd lose you both.

JANICE

Your hat sinks beneath
summer waves ... no space between
here and gone for good.

The Road Home to Arkansas

When mesquite trees whisper names and
beloved faces enter   dreams—
it's time to go home.

Road winds over deep-running rivers,
through rice fields, old hills, pastures
of belly-high grass. Ancient strains of hammered
dulcimers echo off high ridges, naked ridges, float
through river valleys, blue-flowered calico.

Grizzled farmers in frayed "gimme" caps still greet
by lifting two fingers from steering wheels of rickety
trucks; women in faded bonnets stoop in gardens
of pole beans, okra, Big Boy tomatoes. White,
clapboard churches nestle among pines and oaks,
steeples sharing the sky with trees. Graveyards'
white headstones look like fields of poppies
in sun; *Amazing Grace* wafts from open doors,
invites breezes and sinners to enter.

I am again in the place I began, land of gentle
people; the slow, soft voices rest easy on this ear.
The road climbs the Ridge to my son's home,
and grandchildren's laughter is strung from trees

—lanterns filled with fireflies, where the world
spills over—with child-blue eyes.

I sink again into the tender care of family
—friends, pick up loose ends
of past conversations and continue
—like reading a novel I never want to finish.

When I leave, I follow the same road home
to sprawling live oaks, Spanish missions,
lemon-yellow Esperanzas, to a man with blue-gray
eyes, who knows the road
always circles back—to him.

Friedrich Park

A tree shadow slants across the trail
        small puffs of dust explode with each foot fall
            moving across tree roots, rock tops
I recall a mountaineer's words
          There are no unimportant steps.

Placing one foot after the other
        judging contours, estimating drop downs and step ups
            feeling a way along scree slopes
I remember a mountaineer's words
          Make each step count.

All this long hot summer
        hiking the trails of Friedrich Park I learn my lesson
            there is only the next step
and you here walking beside me
          Every step counting.

Whores and Horse Thieves

Every family has a whore or horse thief in the bone
closet. Grandmother's family kept them shut

away——   scandal camped in the den,
blinds drawn, feasting on   forbidden fruit;

family members tiptoed around—as if
such secrets did not exist. Only Aunt Willa's rolled eyes

or behind-the-hand whispers—indicated betrayal.

When scandal moved into this family's house—
            I quietly bore the village

gossip—heads turned when I entered a room;
conversations halted at my approach.

Humiliation—more feeling than I thought I could bear.

But I clutched dignity in these fists,
held my head like a wired rose.

Years later, I watch with round eyes—hand-on-mouth

as Jerry Springer opens closets to craning crowds,
reveals whores in stained dresses, horse thieves
with nooses, invites guests on stage to point—and yell.

I wonder how   it might feel to stand   on stage,
            throw a chair, howl

the full-throated rage of a wounded animal.
Could vindication come   from the chanting crowd—

public shaming—of whore and thief?

JANICE

Betrayal

Surprised, I look down
see the knife handle rotate
feel trust bleeding out.

Denial

Truths gather, unspoken, on back of tongue
so jagged they must be held   lightly,
balanced, to keep from the spill of recognition.

We can't admit to shame,
ragged scarlet—purple
citron on edge.

Nor can we own guilt—
futile swallowing—burning
the back of our throats.

We hide from fear,
white eyes in the dark—
desperately seeking—light
—where no candle burns.

Let us not feel a heart pulled from mooring
indelible blood across the surface,
oil spill on water, insidious

Denial   good and faithful servant   makes possible
the holding and balance—

*Presenting the Amazing
New Cleansing Discovery—*

HONESTY!

Shake a little into the corners of your
mind and you'll be amazed at the results!
Within minutes you'll see its active
ingredients go to work destroying fears
and dissolving those hard-to-remove insecurities.
Your mind will be left sparkling clean and
free of doubt …

HONESTY—try some today!

Make your mind a place *you'd* like to live.

Beach Time

It's time for us to get to a beach again
with its salve
of waves
rolling in
        out
over the soul
          under the cares
laying it all down   differently
amidst the salt-flecked foam.

Norfork

She approaches the lake of her childhood, strains to catch
first glimpse of water against the light. Today we cross on
bridge—ferries retired long ago, but lake still lies in a bed
of deep valleys. Oak-studded mountains rise from shore.

~ ~ ~

Impatient to be on the lake. Her body knifes the surface.
Water wraps around her—deep balm. Lake flows over.
Under. Around. Part of her wants to remain under water.
Part of her—reaches for sky. Mountain air fills the lungs.
Sunlight. The powerful strokes bring her back to us—
waiting beside the boat.

~ ~ ~

Reckless, we wear wigs the quiet one brought. Apply tattoos.
Pose. Strut. Hold in stomachs. Ask strangers to take our
picture. After lunch, we sprawl. Sated. Younger at sixty
than we've ever been. Cell phone rings. She answers.
Listens. She was waiting for this.

~ ~ ~

We call the dragon by name, tap into it, breathe fire—
with her. What if we built an effigy? Air around her—still
smolders. We chant as she fashions it. A bald head. Beady
eyes behind glasses. Seamless mouth.

A chorus of cheers, each woman crouches over the
effigy—streams hiss, spirals of steam rise. We tumble into
the lake. Cleansed. Empowered women. Young. Wild.
Laughing again.

Part 5
ENDINGS AND BEGINNINGS

Miscarriage at Six Months, 1971

The contractions began during our Las Vegas Casino
Night. The Elk's Club. Much anticipated evening of
gambling. Drinking. I left, speaking the words my
husband wanted—to hear—*Stay—I'll be OK.*

Curled up in my bed, rocking you through the scared,
cat-squalling hours—until he came. I moved to a chair
in the den and crouched there, arms wrapped around
my legs, rocking you in waters. Cramps turned—to labor.
I whispered, *Not yet.*

After hours. I waited to call—until light. I left a note
and drove us to St. Bernard's Catholic Hospital, one
hand on the wheel, the other—cradled and stroked you.
I wondered why you didn't kick—and hoped you slept—
but at the hospital, doctor said—you were dead.

Nuns did not allow doctors to take fetuses, even dead—
I was put in a bed. I labored long. Family gathered. Dad
held Mom upright—when I grabbed the headboard bars,
begged for something. The nurse said, "You're only six
months along. You shouldn't be—in this much pain."

Afternoon sun slanted through blinds, leaving tired shadows
on hospital-green walls. I knew you were coming, felt your

small body slip from mine. An easy sensation, like my husband sliding from me.

Doctor strode in, lifted the sheet. Flipped it back. And looked at you, hands on his hips—*A little boy,* he said. *A perfect little boy.* Then with one hand, he reached inside, tore your silky red bed from this body, sucked his teeth—while nuns briskly gathered you up, you—and the bloody sheets—an embarrassment, it seemed, to be spirited away.

Our small-town doctor, who pledged to *Do No Harm* turned— to walk from the room. Paused. Then looked back at me— and said—*You really messed up—this time.*

Grief

primroses
are a field of pink faces
each pointing to the setting sun

except for one clump
beneath a tree
like a family
shadowed by grief
these flowers
face the morning
the last direction
they knew the light

After the Suicide of Sally's Son

Following a distant, difficult journey,
I pull into Emerson Mortuary's lot.
Friend of forty years
mourns the loss of a second son.
I'm praying for words   to bring small solace
      strength   to be
a pillar—palpable beside her.

Something makes me look—
a fiery autumn Bradford pear, heart-shaped
velveteen leaves—
Red in morning sun, gentle breeze.

I breathe deeply   smile.
      Yes—   thank you for reminding me.
      You are here.
I am   soft,   open,   strong,
a bulwark should my friend need.

If she asks,
      Where was God when my son pulled the trigger?

I will be able to embrace her—answer,
      Holding him   and grieving his terrible choice.

JANICE

Little Death

A phone call on a Sunday afternoon
takes my husband's breath away
unexpected news
opens a chasm in his heart
through which an old friend
disappears.

I knew the man who died
although we were not close.
Even so
his life flashed before my eyes
I felt the void in my future
where he could not be grasped
and saw him fade to history
in an instant.

Disbelief. Regret. Futures no longer possible.
Memories of all that was.

A little death. A dry run.
A dress rehearsal for the day
my own heart cracks.

William Says Goodbye

He enters—holding Ma's hand. Does not shrink from sight and sound—his grandmother thrashing, despite morphine. Instead, he climbs on the bed, places a tiny hand on hers— and pats—comforting the only way he knows.

For the first time in days, she stops struggling. Opens the eyes. Smiles.

Restive, the small boy cries to go outside. He flutters around the pool, a fledgling learning to trust wings. Summer heat broken. The air, breathable. Beyond words, his grandfather sits on step, gazes without sight. William pauses. Sits beside him. And again—that small hand reaches out—placed on the old man's knee, content to give—quiet company.

Back in the bedroom, he spots his toy stereo, clamors to play. His mother turns the knob and the gentle strains of *A Child's Prayer* begin. Music seeks dark corners, drifts, straightens sad bones.

William sits quietly on the floor. Legs crossed. Looking at his book. His last birthday cake held one candle.

The Phoenix That Rises

Toward the end of the year
    she died twice.

The first time,
    she died after running through the labyrinth
    of a health care system
    that let her father drop over an edge
    and fall beyond saving.

The second time,
    she died after racing halfway across Texas
    to reach the other half of her heart,
    his time bomb of diabetes
    exploding in his brain.

At the end of the year,
    she had piles of ashes
    over which she struggled to
    resurrect a life, searching for
    the girl she was.

But the part of the story
they forget to tell you is this:

    The phoenix that rises
    is not the same phoenix
    that dies.

In the final days

of my uncle's life   I sit beside the bed,
hold   his cooling hand   in this warm one.

Bone ache so deep
                    morphine fails—

he whispers over   and over
    Help me. Please help me.

For fifty years   he shared
this bed   with Mother's sister—

the body's slight impression
                              still   in the mattress.

Her death—
sudden   overwhelming   loss.
His—   will be   a release.

And then   into the silence of the room
            he says

No one   knows   where the heart sits.

The Last Heartbeat

Caballo Blanco ran
out of heartbeats
beside a mountain stream
in the Gila Wilderness of New Mexico.

Heartbeats had powered him
away from a cave in Hawaii
and a love lost,
down tens of thousands of miles of trails

Colorado, Guatemala, Mexico,
to the Copper Canyons of the Tarahumara
to his third naming
to fame.

And on and on he ran to his final heartbeat
alone, beside a mountain stream
the wild air in his mouth
an unfamiliar silence in his ears.

When the raven's wing

sweeps lightly over my body
this tired mantle sloughs away like a locust's shell,
lifting the smoky shadow from these tired bones,
revealing the Light that is mine alone

        in a way unimagined,
like the blind woman, who snips
    threads sewn to eyelids,
and slowly opens eyes long-sealed—
    beholds herself for the first time,
radiant   whole.

The Divine dwells in me
                and it lives in you,
gives me strength to live,
Grace to hold my faith
        through the last, long journey.

Late Afternoon

After industrious striving
And before the moon's slow spin among the stars

Late afternoon's uncertainty.
Am I arriving, or departing?

Shall I continue to collect life's gewgaws and gimcracks
Or count what has been abandoned?

I see only this: At the end, night will come
And the moon's silver light—full, half, crescent

Will chill skin to feathers
In preparation for the final flight.

The Bottle Tree

Round Top, Texas

Follow the garden path, turn
a corner—at the ramshackle
greenhouse   prepare to startle
out of your lethargy   then
behold colors   flashing in noon light.

Remains of an ancient cedar,
wood bleached to powder grey,
lit with empty bottles
recycled from a garbage heap,
secured   upside down   at crazy angles
on branches   and six-inch nails.

The bottles, a Vegas strip
of colors   azure blue, Cardinal
red, sea-foam green, doubloon gold.

Scattered among the shouting colors are clear,
crystalline bottles, the undulating necks—
A humble Coke. Arizona green tea.

Right then   and there, I thought
Forget about cremation—

when I die, I want to be a Bottle Tree!
Plant my bones straight-up   in Texas
soil, raise one leg, flex the foot, and spread
these toes   so all five can hold
a bottle—place cobalt bottles in my sockets
that I might finally have blue eyes,
fill this hole   in my head
with a bottle brilliant and   ingenious.

Stick a bottle on each rib bone
that children might play a riff

                                        with silver spoons.

Stretch my arms toward the universe,
place Hallelujah bottles   on each finger.

JANICE

Laughing

When it is my turn

To come around again

I will laugh and laugh

Because as much as I will want

To remember everything

When stepping across the threshold

To my new life

I will remember nothing

And in forgetting

Get to learn it all again

Laughing.

Part 6
WILD THINGS

JANICE

Earth Day 2008

The professor steps up to the podium
and delivers his black-and-white PowerPoint presentation
stuffed with bullet points and
sub-bullet points and sub-sub-bullet points
discussing nature writers from Thoreau
through Burroughs, and Krutch, and Carson
until the audience yearns for one green thing
          one fact fallen off a timeline
one stray thought meandering across the hierarchy …

          … when the professor's attention is diverted by a noise
on the lectern where he is startled to find a rattlesnake
rustling among his notes.

No matter. He knows his material by heart. Except
he is momentarily distracted by
a mother javelina and her three little ones tap-tapping
all in a line toward him from stage left. After which,
he notices the projection screen is undulating just a bit
and before long, a few, then many, then thousands
of free-tailed bats are escaping from behind the screen,
over the heads of the audience, out an exit door,
          and into the dusk.

Well.
The professor clears his throat,

turns back to his neatly organized presentation
when from the corner of an eye he spies a white-tailed deer
peeping around the edge of a stage curtain while in the far shadows
a cougar crouches, shoulders up beside its ears,
tail slowly circling in the air, considering the possibilities.

At just this moment,
a large bullfrog squatting center stage lets out a croak
and is soon joined by others from backstage,
in stairwells, and in otherwise empty seats until a
stirring cacophony fills the hall.

In the darkness above
a barn owl perches on a girder, head swiveling,
on the lookout for a meal among the field mice scampering
between the feet of attendees.

An occasional yelp from the audience marks a too-close
encounter with the honeybee swarm overhead.

        All too soon,
the time allotted for this presentation
is over. The audience gets up,
some patting into place bat-blown hair,
and leaves well satisfied.

The professor, meanwhile,
backs slowly out of the spotlight, leaving
his dry notes to the rattlesnake.
His PowerPoint presentation lies dead
on the screen, the victim of too many self-inflicted
bullet points.

The Kenai Peninsula of Alaska

We slogged through the flooded woods, attempted to keep
glacier water from spilling into knee-high boots,
lowing   *Yo! Bear!*   with each extra breath.

We stood on the beach—waiting to enter the salt grass.
John, our guide, signaled—and we dropped to one knee;
tongues swelled in our mouths as we waited.

Twenty feet away, dark, round ears slowly rose above
a felled, ancient tree—a boar grizzly bear
lifted his head to peer, myopically, at the animal arrivals.

We were well-trained; no one scattered   or screamed.
A sea breeze blew music through our hair.
A second pair of ears appeared   and a sow

rose to frisk us with her nose—John fingered
his only weapon; a flare at his waist.
Silence, the only sound until
the grizzlies dropped behind the log—continued—mating.

Gray Ghost

The impact reverberates through the house. White-wing
dove lies on deck, head limp, pale blue-gray eyelids—closed.
Ghost etched on plate glass in pale gray—widespread wings,
individual breast, tail feathers, foot prints, head slanted—
open beak, a bit of tongue, even its eye-print. Could any
bird survive?

I give thanks for this creature. When my husband and I
wake, we lie listening to doves. In evening, even as we reach
for the other, we hear them call, rustling in the live oak.

Is this the one we rescued from the feeder—his head caught
in metal noose? Or is it the one we watched after it fell from
the walnut tree?

I turn from the window. My eye catches—a small
movement—dove eyes slowly opening, closing. After a
few moments, he raises his head, settles on pink feet. I sit
on floor to watch, will him to survive. He rests, then slowly
shuffles to protecting shade of peace lily, where he sits—
patient as only wild things can be.

I slip away to let the dog inside. I return. The dove is gone.
I cast about, he must have found wits and wings. I stand
a long time looking at the gray ghost on the window.

Birdwatching

Really
it looked quite easy
a simple jump
two wings forward to take the air
      and up

Wildflower Garden

Next spring new
           bluebonnets
           poppies
           primroses—
Children of bees and butterflies
will collect and scatter—pollen.
Martins will return to same houses,
gorge on insects, raise their young—

In soft light of long days,
I will crouch among the wildflowers,
      wisdom   within all.

JANICE

First Flowers

Of course a dandelion,
already gone to seed

mustards, india and rocket,
old friends from last year

shepherd's purse,
waving valentines

henbit washing across fields
in a purple foam

a first pink primrose
peeking out

baby blue-eyes
blinking in the sun

a shy Missouri violet
hanging low in a shaded glade
its pretty face
redemption enough.

Gray Sky Mourning

My eyes open. Early dawn,
South Texas gray sky morning.

Throwing covers aside, I pad silently
on bare feet, step out onto deck—
                                out into rain.

Count sixty-one days since last storm.
Forty days over one-hundred-degrees
—sun pinned to sky.

Pittosporums died—leaves
on Eve's necklace yellowed, dropped
like petals on a grave.

Red pentas—bloody wounds
on drooping stems. Mexican heather
—stick bundles in dirt. Even the mango
hibiscus forgot to bloom.

I look into gray sky
remembering all that is lost—
lift hands and turn
in holy ceremony,

feeling rain's benediction
soak into this body—a second skin.

Yesterday, shoes left footprints
in the grass—too sharp for bare feet.
Descending stairs today, I step slowly

onto grass;
blades beg
forgiveness.

Holly ferns
sway to secret
rhythm of rain.

Blue-bleached-to-white plumbagos
guzzle water like desert travelers.
A Gerbera daisy swells in my hand.
Rain streaks the dust

on hot pink face
—painted woman   redeemed.

Drought

In this season of drought
only the hardy survive.
Prickly poppies
bindweed
nightshade
stare in to the sun.

The land is burned brown.
Pastures are dirt.

"Not since the great Dust Bowl ..."
"Hottest month on record ..."

The land cracks.
The farmer stands
beneath his blue bowl of sky
squints in to the sun
his roots too deep
to let go yet.

Common Sulphur

On the road, gold bullion reflects
morning sun—
flightless butterfly clings
to oblivion's edge.

*Has fairy dust been brushed
from wings?*
I carefully place butterfly
in cupped palm

where it sways, folded wings,
gripping skin tightly—
even the Gulf breeze

fails to dislodge.   Black
antennae wave, as though
conducting some symphony—music

—sea song of salt air.
I spread her gold wings—
reveal black lace edge
single spot of orange
on each hindwing

small black spot
on forewings.
Is it possible   such a creature
is named Common   Sulphur?

She alone should be   called *Butterfly.* I shield
from wind   feel her in my palm—
light as an empty wren's egg.

Her body hums.

Delicate black
legs loosen their grip.
I give her back to wind—
and the edges of the world

fall away.

JANICE

Flower opening:
butterfly attends, moving
wings in slow applause.

Snow in Summer

after the tropical storm

Hermine blew
—drenched
dry   San Antonio

took out the top of an old elm—
broke off   a large limb
from an ancient mesquite
which   I am sure   has hosted

Indians   mission friars   German
settlers   under fragile shade—

I am not sure   how it missed the house.
Thirty thousand homes without

power—   ninety degrees and counting.
My husband and I—   tough, resilient

—opened windows   counted blessings
          went out   to eat.

And then   rain lilies
appeared—   the way they do

amidst the wreck   six tiny, white petals
arranged like the Star   of David

around miniature white stamens, yellow
pistils   mindless

of boundaries   ill mannered   glorious

            they blanket the grass and weeds alike
                            with white

                        Snow   in summer.

The Wild Bunch

A spring day
on a well-manicured college campus
and I am hurrying to the science building
past expanses of grass trimmed
with mathematical precision
      —when I am stopped in my tracks
by a flourish of wild primroses
bursting from the edge of a lawn,
tended as lovingly as prize-winning roses
or rare orchids,
pink merrymaking allowed
in the midst of green geometry
proof that one groundskeeper
has properly calculated
the dimensions of the human heart.

Kiko, Dancing with Leaves

Dressed against the chill.
Knit cap. Flannel shirt.
No top hat and tails—

Kiko blows autumn leaves.

Buttery elm, ash,
Texas redbud
fly
like gold coins tossed
from
a benevolent hand.

The blower is part of that
body; Kiko leaps, twirls, tosses
his head   until loosened hair   glints
like obsidian
under early   tamed   sun.

Heedless of
                    tired legs   damaged elbow,

Kiko and the tawny leaves
dance—   October's first morning.

JANICE

Shuffling through dead leaves
one suspends and flies away—
last summer butterfly.

Who needs Christmas lights—
fall leaves twinkle all the way
in to December.

Winter wind blows in
extinguishing the lit trees
in a rain of leaves.

Part 7
LAST WORDS

Patina

A quiet girl with thick lenses,
hair and eyes the color of earth.
A *Coke* gone flat in a family of blue-eyed blondes.

When she was one day old, her father
asked, *Can you fix her nose?*
He expected, though never received,
perfection—she learned to trim herself to fit.

The ideal mate: a charming man,
fond of black label Jack
Daniels, aces and kings—women
who spread legs—When her son

drew attention away from him, ridicule
and long absences—became her husband's
tools of choice, spurring her to try
harder—When she looked

at what was left, little
remained—and still she failed to please;
one day—she buried the blade,
reached for a discarded wood chip that read

This Is Not My Fault; it didn't fit,
exactly—into its old spot—
bailing wire held it awhile.
She picked up, reapplied *I'm Intelligent,*

then found *My Opinion Counts.*
She realized his voice didn't matter.

Sixty-eight years of summers—
and she still has that same nose.

Her hair is white. She loves a man
who looks into her. Sometimes,
she sands rough edges, planes a knot
because it pleases her to—
a soft patina reflects the light.

Wild Poem

Write a wild poem

> *a poem*
>> *about leaping*
>>> *without a net*

> *a poem*
>> *about stepping into the woods*
>>> *with no guarantee*
>>>> *of coming out alive*

> *a poem*
>> *about diving into an ocean with*
>>> *waves so high and wild*
>>>> *they block the sun for days*
> *or years*

there will be no promises in this poem
not of survival   nor sense   nor salvation

only

> *that your companion will be*
>> *your own*
>>> *true*
>>>> *self.*

Silence: A Meditation

I

A fawn hidden in the forest. Wrens waiting for mother's return. Elephant herd moving through Zimbabwe jungle.

II

Bluebonnets spiked with Indian paintbrush. Seed bursts, root surges down for sustenance, stem stretches toward light.

III

Trumpeter swan flown off course. Fireflies. Fetus floating in a womb. Vultures riding summer thermals. Meteors streaking to earth. A Spoonbill's breast feather flying again on breeze. Cloud shadows racing. A candled egg.

IV

Fire ants in a mound. Garden spider biding time on edge of web. Unfaithful heart. An obituary page. Global warming. Our old dog closing eyes for the last time. Alligator as it waits for lunch, eyes above water. Alcohol and Father's liver. Cancer consuming Mother's bones.

V

Your hand holding mine. Our home after grandchildren
leave. Message passed between your eyes and mine. Heat
lightning. Goodbye tears staining grandson's face. Napping
on sofa, news spread across face. Edge of daydream
painted in pinks.

VI

Lunar eclipse. Candle pushing back the dark. Our Blue
Planet seen from space. Sunburned summer evening. Jet
streams striping turquoise sky. The Pleiades, Big Dipper,
and Orion strung like fairy lights across the Milky Way.

VII

Viet Nam Memorial—58,178 names carved in black
granite. A mother in search of a son. The ovens at Dachau.
Pile of shoes in Holocaust Museum, Washington, D.C.
Abandoned slave cabins on Mulberry Row—Monticello.
The homeless—rag piles sleeping in doorways on
Commerce Street.

VIII

A river wandering countryside—seen from thirty thousand
feet. Heat waves shimmering above Chihuahuan Desert.
Kivas at Mesa Verde. Deep aqua blue headwaters of the
Medina River. Blue television screen seen from street.
Pictographs—red, white hands—at Canyon de Chelly.
Alaskan wilderness dressed in millishades of blue. White.

IX

The empty cross. Mission chapel at El Presidio de la Bahia
on Monday afternoon. Ancient totem in Alaskan rainforest.
Sun seeping—into cold bones. Lazy plume of white smoke
rising from campfire. Snow falling on snow.

Sacred

a poem of remembering

You are a sacred site.
I am a sacred site.

Face-to-face
at any place in this wide world
the sacred
is in the presence of
the sacred
is in the presence of
the sacred.

How we might shine,
each in to the other.
What could we not accomplish?
What darkness could stand
against the light of such a sun.

Gift

Gray light creeps in around curtain's edge. Our dog walks the ridge of my body, carefully picking his way, scattering dream sleep—as he would disperse sea gulls on the beach.

I know nothing about—what the day holds—giving into inevitability, I stagger into clothes, remember my hat, slip out into Gulf Coast dawn, dog dancing like a kite on the end of his leash. Wet before reaching the beach road, I nod to the wisdom of walking early.

The sun has yet to break—a Great Blue Heron is already fishing. Except for his cape ruffling in the breeze, he is motionless—yellow, rebar legs planted in shallow water, snake-like neck coiled to strike, terrible eyes narrowed. Focused.

I look to the right—there—hovering just above the tops of Coast live oaks—a harvest moon glows pale—against the lightening sky.

Quick glance over the water tells me the sun is only minutes away. Looking west, east, I wonder if the moon will wait—

Just then, the bonfire of dawn. Sea and sky turn to red—liquid gold—I stand for a moment, alone in the universe, arms lifted. Palms up—

Moon slides below tree line; sun firefights its way through last clouds. I pet my good dog, turn toward home—

JANICE

Tide's Turn

Now comes the exhale
that glorious run of the tide
racing toward the full moon,
its back lit with the way home.

ACKNOWLEDGMENTS

The authors are grateful to the editors of the following publications in which versions of some of these poems first appeared.

Janice Rebecca Campbell

The Dreamcatcher: "Friedrich Park," "Grief," "I Could Have Stars in All My Poems," "The Wild Bunch"

Passager: "Tide's Turn"

San Antonio Express-News: "Drought," "Lessons in Love Learned Watching Pee Wee Football Practice," "Sacred"

Toni Heringer Falls

The Dreamcatcher: "Arrowhead," "Ice Storm in San Antonio," "Tell Me"

San Antonio Express-News: "Love Song," "Small Sounds" (originally published as "Whispering in the Morning"), "Snow in Summer"

Sustaining Abundant Life: Women's Prayer and Poetry: "After the Suicide of Sally's Son," "When the raven's wing"

Texas Poetry Calendar: "From a Distance," "Goodbye Died in My Mouth" (originally published as "Racing Tornadoes")

Voices Along the River: "Coast Live Oaks," "Common Sulphur," "Gift," "Gray Ghost," "Gray Sky Mourning," "Kiko, Dancing with Leaves," "William Says Goodbye," "Wisdom"

CONTINUED ON NEXT PAGE

Grateful acknowledgment is made to the estate of Yousuf Karsh for permission to reprint his quote on page 54.

Special thanks to Elizabeth and Bob Lende, whose back yard provided an inspirational location for our cover photographs, and to Frank Garcia for his meticulous groundskeeping.

ABOUT THE AUTHORS

Janice Rebecca Campbell is a poet, photographer, and graphic designer. Janice's poems have appeared in anthologies and publications, and she is the author of three other volumes of poetry: *pink merrymaking allowed in the midst of green geometry: Ah: 31 Days • 31 Poems;* and *A Disturbance in the Field: Collected Poems.*

Toni Heringer Falls is a retired teacher, psychotherapist, and an inactive Licensed Professional Counselor. Toni's poetry has been published in numerous anthologies and publications and her poem "Gift" won first place in the San Antonio Poetry Fair, 2010. Toni has completed a manuscript entitled *Snow in Summer* and is seeking a publisher.

Made in United States
Cleveland, OH
01 April 2025

15702532R00090